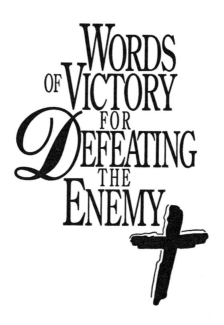

WORDS OF VICTORY FOR DEFEATING THE ENEMY

Creation House
Altamonte Springs, Florida

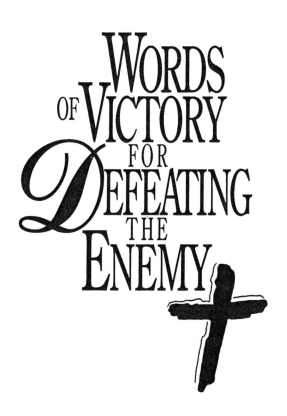

WORDS OF VICTORY FOR DEFEATING THE ENEMY

Creation House
Altamonte Springs Florida

Creation House
Strang Communications Company
190 N. Westmonte Drive
Altamonte Springs, FL 32714
(407) 869-5005

Unless otherwise noted, all Scripture in this book is taken from
the King James Version of the Bible. Verses marked Amplified
are from the Amplified New Testament; copyright © 1954, 1958,
1987 by the Lockman Foundation; used by permission. Scripture marked NASB is from the New American Standard Bible;
copyright © 1960, 1962, 1963, 1968, 1971, 1972, 1973, 1975,
1977 by the Lockman Foundation; used by permission. Scripture marked NEB is from The New English Bible; copyright the
Delegates of the Oxford University Press and the Syndics of the
Cambridge University Press, 1961, 1970; reprinted by permission. Verses marked NIV are from the Holy Bible, New International Version; copyright © 1973, 1978, 1984, International Bible
Society; used by permission. Scripture marked RSV is from the
Revised Standard Version Bible; copyright © 1946, 1952, 1971
by the Division of Christian Education of the National Council
of the Churches of Christ in the USA; used by permission. Verses
marked TLB are from The Living Bible; copyright © 1971 owned
by assignment by Illinois Regional Bank N.A. (as trustee); used
by permission of Tyndale House Publishers Inc., Wheaton, IL
60189; all rights reserved.

E.S. Caldwell, associate editor of Ministries Today, *compiled
this book.*

Contents

PART ONE

Know the Identity of Your Enemy

I. Know the Names of the Enemy of
   God's Children 11

II. Know the Works of Your Enemy 19

III. Evil Spirits Are Fighting Against
   God's People 33

IV. Angels Are Limited in Their Power 38

PART TWO

Know What to Do and Say
to Defeat the Enemy

I. Always Wear the Entire Armor
   God Provides 43

II. Deal Directly With Demonic Forces 50

III. Steps for Deliverance 54

PART THREE

Know That Angels Are Involved in Defeating the Enemy

I. What the Scriptures Teach About Obtaining the Help of Angels 63

II. What the Scriptures Say About the Origin of Angels 69

III. What the Scriptures Say About Angels' Characteristics and Activities 71

IV. What the Scriptures Say About the Appearance of Angels 81

V. What the Scriptures Say About the Titles of Angels 95

VI. What the Old Testament Says About the Activity of Angels in Human Lives 99

VII. What the Gospels Say About the Activity of Angels in the Life of Jesus 125

VIII. What the New Testament Says About the Activity of Angels in Human Lives 131

Introduction

Whether you want to admit it or not, you are on a battlefield. The nation may be at peace but there's a war going on, and you have been targeted by a sometimes subtle, sometimes fierce, always determined enemy—an enemy that assigns his agents to the task of destroying you. This warfare pits the devil and all his hosts against the people of God.

You need not fear this enemy that threatens you or the afflictions he sends your way. If your faith is focused on God, if you find your security in Christ, if you are filled with His powerful Spirit, you do not have to live in fear. God does not leave you alone to face the onslaughts of evil.

On the other hand, this battle need not be viewed as one of dodging fiery darts and evading hidden booby traps. Jesus is the Lord of hosts. He expects you to enlist by His side, engage the enemy and win battle after battle. The Lord is with you to lead you to victory! Ministering angels are assigned to watch over you—they too are engaged in an ongoing conflict with the forces of hell.

Our great commander-in-chief has provided His recruits with a manual for warfare, the Holy Bible. Everything in this handbook comes from that great source book. In it you will discover how to identify your enemy, although these agents of the devil slink among us in clever disguises. You will learn their names. Their *modus operandi* is exposed. You will discover their multiple methods of operation, their wide range of terrorist strategies.

And unlike any other handbook on warfare, this one spells out the limitations and the certain defeat of Satan and his minions.

It is tragic that so many Christians suffer defeat in their day-to-day struggles against the forces of the enemy. There is a way to live in which you are equipped and empowered to tear down the devil's strongholds and put his demons to flight. This handbook points out the armor God has provided for His soldiers. It tells you how to engage in warfare and win as you contest the invisible evil spirits seeking the destruction of both the unconverted and your fellow believers who are weak. It guides you step by step in bringing deliverance to anyone afflicted by satanic schemes.

God Himself has an invisible army at least twice the size and tremendously more powerful than everything that Satan can muster. This handbook tells you how to obtain the help of heaven's angelic army. It describes their appearance and their characteristics, and it traces the many references to their activities in human lives throughout the pages of Scripture.

With all this going for those who enlist on the Lord's side, how can they do anything but win?

All the Bible verses in this book are from the King James Version, but in a number of instances, some clarity can be gained from phrases from other Bible translations. When this is the case, the alternate translation follows the verse.

—E.S. Caldwell

PART ONE

Know the Identity of Your Enemy

For we wrestle not against flesh and blood, but against principalities, against powers, against the rulers of the darkness of this world, against spiritual wickedness in high places.

Ephesians 6:12

I. Know the Names of the Enemy of God's Children

Called the serpent

Now the serpent was more subtil than any beast of the field which the Lord God had made. And he said unto the woman, Yea, hath God said, Ye shall not eat of every tree of the garden? And the woman said unto the serpent, We may eat of the fruit of the trees of the garden: but of the fruit of the tree which is in the midst of the garden, God hath said, Ye shall not eat of it, neither shall ye touch it, lest ye die.

Genesis 3:1-5

Called Lucifer, son of the morning

How art thou fallen from heaven, O Lucifer, son of the morning! how art thou cut down to the ground, which didst weaken the nations! For thou hast said in thine heart, I will ascend into heaven, I will exalt my throne above the stars of God: I will sit also upon the mount of the congregation, in the sides of the north: I will ascend above the heights of the clouds; I will be like the most High. Yet thou shalt be brought down to hell, to the sides of the pit. They that see thee shall narrowly look upon thee, and consider thee, saying, Is this the man that made the earth to tremble, that did shake kingdoms; that made the world as a wilderness, and destroyed the cities thereof; that opened not the house of his prisoners? All the kings of the nations, even all of them, lie in glory, every one in his own house. But thou art cast out of thy grave like an abominable branch, and as the raiment of those that are slain, thrust through with a sword, that go down to the stones of the pit; as a carcase trodden under feet. Thou shalt not be joined with them in burial, because thou hast destroyed thy land, and slain thy people: the seed of evildoers shall never be renowned.

Isaiah 14:12-20

Called Satan

And Satan stood up against Israel, and provoked David to number Israel.

1 Chronicles 21:1

Called the anointed cherub

Moreover the word of the Lord came unto me, saying, Son of man, take up a lamentation upon the king of Tyrus, and say unto him, Thus saith the Lord God; Thou sealest up the sum, full of wisdom, and perfect in beauty. Thou hast been in Eden the garden of God; every precious stone was thy covering, the sardius, topaz, and the diamond, the beryl, the onyx, and the jasper, the sapphire, the emerald, and the carbuncle, and gold: the workmanship of

13

thy tabrets and of thy pipes was prepared in
thee in the day that thou wast created.
Thou art the anointed cherub that covereth;
and I have set thee so; thou wast upon the
holy mountain of God; thou hast walked up
and down in the midst of the stones of fire.
Thou wast perfect in thy ways from the day
that thou wast created, till iniquity was
found in thee. By the multitude of thy
merchandise they have filled the midst of
thee with violence, and thou hast sinned:
therefore I will cast thee as profane out of
the mountain of God: and I will destroy
thee, O covering cherub, from the midst of
the stones of fire. Thine heart was lifted up
because of thy beauty, thou hast corrupted
thy wisdom by reason of thy brightness: I
will cast thee to the ground, I will lay thee
before kings, that they may behold thee.
Thou hast defiled thy sanctuaries by the
multitude of thine iniquities, by the iniquity
of thy traffick; therefore will I bring forth a
fire from the midst of thee, it shall devour
thee, and I will bring thee to ashes upon
the earth in the sight of all them that
behold thee. All they that know thee among
the people shall be astonished at thee: thou

shalt be a terror, and never shalt thou be
any more.

Ezekiel 28:11-19

Called the devil

Then was Jesus led up of the Spirit into
the wilderness to be tempted of the devil.

Matthew 4:1

Called the tempter

And when the tempter came to him, he
said, If thou be the Son of God, command
that these stones be made bread.

Matthew 4:3

Called the evil one

And lead us not into temptation, but
deliver us from evil: For thine is the
kingdom, and the power, and the glory, for
ever. Amen.

Matthew 6:13

"The evil one" (NIV)

Called Beelzebub

It is enough for the disciple that he be as
his master, and the servant as his lord. If

they have called the master of the house
Beelzebub, how much more shall they call
them of his household?

Matthew 10:25

Called the wicked one

When any one heareth the word of the
kingdom, and understandeth it not, then
cometh the wicked one, and catcheth away
that which was sown in his heart. This is he
which received seed by the way side.

Matthew 13:19

Called the enemy

The enemy that sowed them is the devil;
the harvest is the end of the world; and the
reapers are the angels.

Matthew 13:39

Called the prince of this world

Now is the judgment of this world: now
shall the prince of this world be cast out.

John 12:31

Called the god of this world

In whom the god of this world hath blinded the minds of them which believe not, lest the light of the glorious gospel of Christ, who is the image of God, should shine unto them.

2 Corinthians 4:4

Called Belial

And what concord hath Christ with Belial? or what part hath he that believeth with an infidel?

2 Corinthians 6:15

Called the prince of the power of the air

And you hath he quickened, who were dead in trespasses and sins; wherein in time past ye walked according to the course of this world, according to the prince of the power of the air, the spirit that now worketh in the children of disobedience.

Ephesians 2:1-2

Called your adversary

Be sober, be vigilant; because your adversary the devil as a roaring lion, walketh about, seeking whom he may devour.

1 Peter 5:8

Called Abaddon and Apollyon

And they had a king over them, which is the angel of the bottomless pit, whose name in the Hebrew tongue is Abaddon, but in the Greek tongue hath his name Apollyon.

Revelation 9:11

Called the accuser of our brethren

And I heard a loud voice saying in heaven, Now is come salvation, and strength, and the kingdom of our God, and the power of his Christ: for the accuser of our brethren is cast down, which accused them before our God day and night.

Revelation 12:10

Called the dragon

And they worshipped the dragon which gave power unto the beast: and they worshipped the beast, saying, Who is like unto the beast? who is able to make war with him?

Revelation 13:4

II. Know the Works of Your Enemy

Undermines belief in what God says

And the serpent said unto the woman, Ye shall not surely die: for God doth know that in the day ye eat thereof, then your eyes shall be opened, and ye shall be as gods, knowing good and evil.

Genesis 3:4-5

Promotes occult abominations

There shall not be found among you any one that maketh his son or his daughter to pass through the fire, or that useth divination, or an observer of times, or an enchanter, or a witch, or a charmer, or a consulter with familiar spirits, or a wizard, or a necromancer. For all that do these things are an abomination unto the Lord: and because of these abominations the Lord thy God doth drive them out from before thee. Thou shalt be perfect with the Lord thy God. For these nations, which thou shalt possess, harkened unto observers of times, and unto diviners: but as for thee, the Lord thy God hath not suffered thee so to do.

Deuteronomy 18:10-14

Provokes people to sin

And Satan stood up against Israel, and provoked David to number Israel....And God was displeased with this thing; therefore he smote Israel.

1 Chronicles 21:1,7

Destroys people's employees and livestock

And the Lord said unto Satan, Behold, all that he hath is in thy power; only upon himself put not forth thine hand. So Satan went forth from the presence of the Lord.

And there was a day when his sons and his daughters were eating and drinking wine in their eldest brother's house: and there came a messenger unto Job, and said, The oxen were plowing, and the asses feeding beside them: And the Sabeans fell upon them, and took them away; yea, they have slain the servants with the edge of the sword; and I only am escaped alone to tell thee. While he was yet speaking, there came also another, and said, The fire of God has fallen from heaven, and hath burned up the sheep, and the servants, and consumed them; and I only am escaped alone to tell thee. While he was yet speaking, there came also another, and said, The Chaldeans made out three bands, and fell upon the camels, and have carried them away, yea, and slain the servants with the edge of the sword; and I only am escaped alone to tell thee.

Job 1:12-17

Kills people's children

While he was yet speaking, there came also another, and said, Thy sons and thy daughters were eating and drinking wine in their eldest brother's house: and, behold, there came a great wind from the wilderness, and smote the four corners of the house, and it fell upon the young men, and they are dead; and I only am escaped alone to tell thee.

Job 1:18-19

21

Has power over specific territories

But the prince of the kingdom of Persia withstood me one and twenty days: but, lo, Michael, one of the chief princes, came to help me; and I remained there with the kings of Persia.

Daniel 10:13

Resists the priests of the Lord

And he shewed me Joshua the high priest standing before the angel of the Lord, and Satan standing at his right hand to resist him. And the Lord said unto Satan, The Lord rebuke thee, O Satan; even the Lord that hath chosen Jerusalem rebuke thee: is not this a brand plucked out of the fire?

Zechariah 3:1-2

Possesses people and afflicts them with evil spirits

And when he was come to the other side into the country of the Gergesenes, there met him two possessed with devils, coming out of the tombs, exceeding fierce, so that no man might pass by that way.

Matthew 8:28

Possesses people and afflicts them with dumbness and blindness

As they went out, behold, they brought to him a dumb man possessed with a devil. And when the devil was cast out, the dumb spake: and the multitudes marvelled, saying, It was never so seen in Israel.

Matthew 9:32-33

Then was brought unto him one possessed with a devil, blind, and dumb: and he healed him, insomuch that the blind and dumb both spake and saw.

Matthew 12:22

Takes away the Word sown in hearts

When any one heareth the word of the kingdom, and understandeth it not, then cometh the wicked one, and catcheth away that which was sown in his heart. This is he which received seed by the way side.

Matthew 13:19

Gives people wrongful things to say

From that time forth began Jesus to shew unto his disciples, how that he must go unto Jerusalem, and suffer many things of

the elders and chief priests and scribes, and
be killed, and be raised again the third day.
Then Peter took him, and began to rebuke
him, saying, Be it far from thee, Lord: this
shall not be unto thee. But he turned, and
said unto Peter, Get thee behind me, Satan:
thou art an offence unto me: for thou
savourest not the things that be of God, but
those that be of men.

Then said Jesus unto his disciples, If
any man will come after me, let him
deny himself, and take up his cross,
and follow me.

Matthew 16:21-24

Binds people with harmful spirits

And, behold, there was a woman which
had a spirit of infirmity eighteen years, and
was bowed together, and could in no wise
lift up herself. And when Jesus saw her, he
called her to him, and said unto her,
Woman, thou art loosed from thine infirmity. And he laid his hands on her: and
immediately she was made straight, and
glorified God. And the ruler of the
synagogue answered with indignation,
because that Jesus had healed on the sabbath day, and said unto the people, There

are six days in which men ought to work:
in them therefore come and be healed, and
not on the sabbath day. The Lord then
answered him, and said, Thou hypocrite,
doth not each one of you on the sabbath
loose his ox or his ass from the stall, and
lead him away to watering? And ought not
this woman, being a daughter of Abraham,
whom Satan hath bound, lo, these eighteen
years, be loosed from this bond on the sabbath day?

Luke 13:11-16

Seduces the Lord's followers to betray Him

Then entered Satan into Judas surnamed
Iscariot, being of the number of the twelve.
And he went his way, and communed with
the chief priests and captains, how he might
betray him unto them. And they were glad,
and covenanted to give him money. And
he promised, and sought opportunity to
betray him unto them in the absence of
the multitude.

Luke 22:3-6

Kills, steals and destroys

The thief cometh not, but for to steal, and to kill, and to destroy: I am come that they might have life, and that they might have it more abundantly.

John 10:10

Tempts believers to cheat and lie

But Peter said, Ananias, why hath Satan filled thine heart to lie to the Holy Ghost, and to keep back part of the price of the land?

Acts 5:3

Oppresses people

How God anointed Jesus of Nazareth with the Holy Ghost and with power: who went about doing good, and healing all that were oppressed of the devil; for God was with him.

Acts 10:38

Twists the right ways of the Lord

And said, O full of all subtilty and all mischief, thou child of the devil, thou enemy of all righteousness, wilt thou not

26

cease to pervert the right ways of the Lord?
Acts 13:10

Possesses people and enables them to predict the future

And it came to pass, as we went to prayer, a certain damsel possessed with a spirit of divination met us, which brought her masters much gain by soothsaying.
Acts 16:16

"By which she predicted the future" (NIV)

Causes the possessed person to attack others

Then certain of the vagabond Jews, exorcists, took upon them to call over them which had evil spirits the name of the Lord Jesus, saying, We adjure you by Jesus whom Paul preacheth. And there were seven sons of one Sceva, a Jew, and chief of the priests, which did so. And the evil spirit answered and said, Jesus I know, and Paul I know; but who are ye? And the man in whom the evil spirit was leaped on them, and overcame them, and prevailed against

them, so that they fled out of that house
naked and wounded.

Acts 19:13-16

Tempts people to sexual sin

Defraud ye not one the other, except it
be with consent for a time, that ye may
give yourselves to fasting and prayer; and
come together again, that Satan tempt you
not for your incontinency.

1 Corinthians 7:5

Seeks to gain an advantage over believers

To whom ye forgive any thing, I forgive
also: for if I forgave any thing, to whom I
forgave it, for your sakes forgave I it in the
person of Christ; lest Satan should get an
advantage of us: for we are not ignorant of
his devices.

2 Corinthians 2:10-11

Blinds the minds of people to the gospel

In whom the god of this world hath
blinded the minds of them which believe
not, lest the light of the glorious gospel of

Christ, who is the image of God, should shine unto them.

2 Corinthians 4:4

Is transformed into an angel of light

And no marvel; for Satan himself is transformed into an angel of light.

2 Corinthians 11:14

Buffets Christians with afflictions

And lest I should be exalted above measure through the abundance of the revelations, there was given to me a thorn in the flesh, the messenger of Satan to buffet me, lest I should be exalted above measure.

2 Corinthians 12:7

Preaches another gospel

But though we, or an angel from heaven, preach any other gospel unto you than that which we have preached unto you, let him be accursed.

Galatians 1:8

Works in the children of disobedience

Wherein in time past ye walked according to the course of this world, according to the prince of the power of the air, the spirit that now worketh in the children of disobedience.

Ephesians 2:2

Hurls fiery darts at God's people

Above all, taking the shield of faith, wherewith ye shall be able to quench all the fiery darts of the wicked.

Ephesians 6:16

Hinders the work of the Lord

Wherefore we would have come unto you, even I Paul, once and again; but Satan hindered us.

1 Thessalonians 2:18

Works signs and lying wonders

Even him, whose coming is after the working of Satan with all power and signs and lying wonders.

2 Thessalonians 2:9

Snares those who do not have a good record

Moreover he must have a good report of them which are without; lest he fall into reproach and the snare of the devil.

1 Timothy 3:7

Teaches false restrictions and wrong doctrines

Now the Spirit speaketh expressly, that in the latter times some shall depart from the faith, giving heed to seducing spirits, and doctrines of devils; speaking lies in hypocrisy; having their conscience seared with a hot iron; forbidding to marry, and commanding to abstain from meats, which God hath created to be received with thanksgiving of them which believe and know the truth.

1 Timothy 4:1-3

Induces people to turn aside after him

But the younger widows refuse: for when they have begun to wax wanton against Christ, they will marry; having damnation, because they have cast off their first faith. And withal they learn to be idle, wandering

31

about from house to house; and not only idle, but tattlers also and busybodies, speaking things which they ought not. I will therefore that the younger women marry, bear children, guide the house, give none occasion to the adversary to speak reproachfully. For some are already turned aside after Satan.

1 Timothy 5:11-15

Sets snares to entrap people

And that they may recover themselves out of the snare of the devil, who are taken captive by him at his will.

2 Timothy 2:26

Devours and afflicts careless believers

Be sober, be vigilant; because your adversary the devil as a roaring lion, walketh about, seeking whom he may devour: whom resist stedfast in the faith, knowing that the same afflictions are accomplished in your brethren that are in the world.

1 Peter 5:8-9

III. Evil Spirits Are Fighting Against God's People

Familiar spirits

Regard not them that have familiar spirits, neither seek after wizards, to be defiled by them: I am the Lord your God.

Leviticus 19:31

Spirits of jealousy

And the spirit of jealousy come upon him, and he be jealous of his wife, and she be defiled: or if the spirit of jealousy come upon him, and he be jealous of his wife, and she be not defiled.

Numbers 5:14

Lying spirits

Now therefore, behold, the Lord hath put a lying spirit in the mouth of these thy prophets, and the Lord hath spoken evil against thee.

2 Chronicles 18:22

Evil angels

He cast upon them the fierceness of his anger, wrath, and indignation, and trouble, by sending evil angels among them. He made a way to his anger; he spared not their soul from death, but gave their life over to the pestilence; and smote all the firstborn in Egypt; the chief of their strength in the tabernacles of Ham.

Psalm 78:49-51

Spirits of heaviness

To appoint unto them that mourn in Zion, to give unto them beauty for ashes, the oil of joy for mourning, the garment of praise for the spirit of heaviness; that they might be called trees of righteousness, the planting of the Lord, that he might be glorified.

Isaiah 61:3

"A spirit of despair" (NIV)

Spirits of whoredoms

They will not frame their doings to turn unto their God: for the spirit of whoredoms is in the midst of them, and they have not known the Lord

Hosea 5:4

Unclean spirits

And it shall come to pass in that day, saith the Lord of hosts, that I will cut off the names of the idols out of the land, and they shall no more be remembered: and also I will cause the prophets and the unclean spirit to pass out of the land.

Zechariah 13:2

Dumb spirits

And one of the multitude answered and said, Master, I have brought unto thee my son, which hath a dumb spirit.

Mark 9:17

Foul spirits

When Jesus saw that the people came running together, he rebuked the foul spirit, saying unto him, Thou dumb and deaf spirit, I charge thee, come out of him, and enter no more into him.

Mark 9:25

Spirits of unclean devils

And in the synagogue there was a man, which had a spirit of an unclean devil, and cried out with a loud voice.

Luke 4:33

Spirits of infirmity

And, behold, there was a woman which had a spirit of infirmity eighteen years, and was bowed together, and could in no wise lift up herself.

Luke 13:11

Evil spirits

And the man in whom the evil spirit was leaped on them, and overcame them, and prevailed against them, so that they fled out of that house naked and wounded.

Acts 19:16

Spirits of divination

And it came to pass, as we went to prayer, a certain damsel possessed with a spirit of divination met us, which brought her masters much gain by soothsaying.

Acts 16:16

Spirits of bondage

For ye have not received the spirit of bondage again to fear; but ye have received the Spirit of adoption, whereby we cry, Abba, Father.

Romans 8:15

Spirits of the world

Now we have received, not the spirit of the world, but the spirit which is of God; that we might know the things that are freely given to us of God.

1 Corinthians 2:12

Seducing spirits

Now the Spirit speaketh expressly, that in the latter times some shall depart from the faith, giving heed to seducing spirits, and doctrines of devils.

1 Timothy 4:1

Spirits of fear

For God hath not given us the spirit of fear; but of power, and of love, and of a sound mind.

2 Timothy 1:7

Spirits of antichrist

And every spirit that confesseth not that Jesus Christ is come in the flesh is not of God: and this is that spirit of antichrist, whereof ye have heard that it should come; and even now already is it in the world.

1 John 4:3

Spirits of error

We are of God: he that knoweth God heareth us; he that is not of God heareth not us. Hereby know we the spirit of truth, and the spirit of error.

1 John 4:6

IV. Angels Are Limited in Their Power

They are subject to Christ

"The God of our Lord Jesus Christ...set him at his own right hand in the heavenly places, far above all principality, and power, and dominion, and every name that is named, not only in this world, but also in that which is to come...."

Ephesians 1:17,20,21

Blotting out the handwriting of ordinances that was against us, which was contrary to us, and took it out of the way, nailing it to his cross; and having spoiled principalities and powers, he made a shew of them openly, triumphing over them in it.
Colossians 2:14-15

Who is gone into heaven, and is on the right hand of God; angels and authorities and powers being made subject unto him.
1 Peter 3:22

They resist the prayers of God's people but cannot stop them

And he said unto me, O Daniel, a man greatly beloved, understand the words that I speak unto thee, and stand upright: for unto thee am I now sent. And when he had spoken this word unto me, I stood trembling. Then said he unto me, Fear not, Daniel: for from the first day that thou didst set thine heart to understand, and to chasten thyself before thy God, thy words were heard, and I am come for thy words. But the prince of the kingdom of Persia withstood me one and twenty days: but, lo, Michael, one of the chief princes, came to

39

help me; and I remained there with the kings of Persia. Now I am come to make thee understand what shall befall thy people in the latter days: for yet the vision is for many days.

Daniel 10:11-14

They cannot separate believers from the love of God

For I am persuaded, that neither death, nor life, nor angels, nor principalities, nor powers, nor things present, nor things to come, nor height, nor depth, nor any other creature, shall be able to separate us from the love of God, which is in Christ Jesus our Lord.

Romans 8:38-39

They cannot prevail against Christ's church

And I say also unto thee, That thou art Peter, and upon this rock I will build my church; and the gates of hell shall not prevail against it.

Matthew 16:18

They are excluded from heaven

And there was war in heaven: Michael and his angels fought against the dragon; and the dragon fought and his angels, and prevailed not; neither was their place found any more in heaven. And the great dragon was cast out, that old serpent, called the Devil, and Satan, which deceiveth the whole world: he was cast out into the earth, and his angels were cast out with him.

Revelation 12:7-9

They were charged with folly

Behold, he put no trust in his servants; and his angels he charged with folly.

Job 4:18

They were cast down

For if God spared not the angels that sinned, but cast them down to hell, and delivered them into chains of darkness, to be reserved unto judgment....

2 Peter 2:4

They await judgment

And the angels which kept not their first estate, but left their own habitation, he hath reserved in everlasting chains under darkness unto the judgment of the great day.

Jude 6

Then shall he say also unto them on the left hand, Depart from me, ye cursed, into everlasting fire, prepared for the devil and his angels.

Matthew 25:41

PART TWO

Know What to Do and Say to Defeat the Enemy

I. Always Wear the Entire Armor God Provides

Believe that the Lord within you is much greater than any other power in the world

Ye are of God, little children, and have overcome them: because greater is he that is in you, than he that is in the world.

1 John 4:4

Never give the devil an opportunity to defeat you

Be ye angry, and sin not: let not the sun

go down upon your wrath: neither give
place to the devil.

Ephesians 4:26-27

"Give no opportunity to the devil" (RSV)

Do not attempt to withstand demons without the power of God's might

Finally, my brethren, be strong in the
Lord, and in the power of his might.

Ephesians 6:10

Do not omit any part of the armor

Put on the whole armour of God, that ye
may be able to stand against the wiles of
the devil.

Ephesians 6:11

Our struggle is with a system of evil spirits

For we wrestle not against flesh and
blood, but against principalities, against
powers, against the rulers of the darkness of
this world, against spiritual wickedness in
high places.

Ephesians 6:12

"Great evil princes who rule this world"
(TLB)

Our objective is to win

Wherefore take unto you the whole
armour of God, that ye may be able to
withstand in the evil day, and having done
all, to stand.

Ephesians 6:13

You must control your sexual behavior

Stand therefore, having your loins girt
about with truth....

Ephesians 6:14

("Loins," the seat of generative power;
"truth," signifies faithfulness or fidelity—
editor's comment)

And righteousness shall be the girdle of
his loins, and faithfulness the girdle of his
reins.

Isaiah 11:5

But every man is tempted when he is
drawn away of his own lust, and enticed.
Then when lust hath conceived, it bringeth

forth sin: and sin, when it is finished,
bringeth forth death.

James 1:14-15

Marriage is honourable in all, and the bed
undefiled: but whoremongers and adulterers
God will judge.

Hebrews 13:4

But whoso committeth adultery with a
woman lacketh understanding: he that
doeth it destroyeth his own soul.

Proverbs 6:32

You must protect your heart

Having on the breastplate of righteousness.

Ephesians 6:14

"Having put on the breastplate of integrity
and of moral rectitude and right standing
with God" (Amplified)

Keep thy heart with all diligence; for out
of it are the issues of life.

Proverbs 4:23

But of him are ye in Christ Jesus, who of God is made unto us wisdom, and righteousness, and sanctification, and redemption.

1 Corinthians 1:30

You must protect your walk

And your feet shod with the preparation of the gospel of peace.

Ephesians 6:15

For thou hast delivered my soul from death; wilt not thou deliver my feet from falling, that I may walk before God in the light of the living?

Psalm 56:13

But sanctify the Lord God in your hearts: and be ready always to give an answer to every man that asketh you a reason of the hope that is in you with meekness and fear.

1 Peter 3:15

You must take the shield of faith

Above all, taking the shield of faith,

wherewith ye shall be able to quench all the
fiery darts of the wicked.

Ephesians 6:16

He shall cover thee with his feathers, and
under his wings shalt thou trust: his truth
shall be thy shield and buckler.

Psalm 91:4

"His faithful promises are your armor"
(TLB)

You must take the helmet of salvation

And take the helmet of salvation.

Ephesians 6:17

And that, knowing the time, that now it
is high time to awake out of sleep: for now
is our salvation nearer than when we
believed. The night is far spent, the day is
at hand: let us therefore cast off the works
of darkness, and let us put on the armour
of light. Let us walk honestly, as in the day;
not in rioting and drunkenness, not in
chambering and wantonness, not in strife
and envying. But put ye on the Lord Jesus

Christ, and make not provision for the
flesh, to fulfil the lusts thereof.

Romans 13:11-14

Take the sword of the Spirit

And take...the sword of the Spirit, which
is the word of God.

Ephesians 6:17

"The sword that the Spirit wields"
(Amplified)

For the word of God is quick, and powerful, and sharper than any twoedged sword,
piercing even to the dividing asunder of
soul and spirit, and of the joints and mar-
row, and is a discerner of the thoughts and
intents of the heart.

Hebrews 4:12

I have written unto you, fathers, because
ye have known him that is from the beginning. I have written unto you, young men,
because ye are strong, and the word of God
abideth in you, and ye have overcome the
wicked one.

1 John 2:14

"The Word of God is [always] abiding in you (in your hearts), and you have been victorious over the wicked one" (Amplified)

Prayer is the ultimate weapon

Praying always with all prayer and supplication in the Spirit, and watching thereunto with all perseverance and supplication for all saints.

Ephesians 6:18

"Pray on every occasion in the power of the Spirit" (NEB)

II. Deal Directly With Demonic Forces

Accept your commission from the Lord

And these signs shall follow them that believe; In my name shall they cast out devils; they shall speak with new tongues.

Mark 16:17

Seek the gift of discerning of spirits

For to one is given by the Spirit...discerning of spirits.

1 Corinthians 12:8,10

Beloved, believe not every spirit, but try the spirits whether they are of God: because many false prophets are gone out into the world. Hereby know ye the Spirit of God: Every spirit that confesseth that Jesus Christ is come in the flesh is of God: and every spirit that confesseth not that Jesus Christ is come in the flesh is not of God: and this is that spirit of antichrist, whereof ye have heard that it should come; and even now already is it in the world.

1 John 4:1-3

You must have spiritual strength greater than the demon

I can do all things through Christ which strengtheneth me.

Philippians 4:13

The finger of God is stronger than any demon

And the Lord said unto Moses, Say unto

Aaron, Stretch out thy rod, and smite the dust of the land, that it may become lice throughout all the land of Egypt. And they did so; for Aaron stretched out his hand with his rod, and smote the dust of the earth, and it became lice in man, and in beast; all the dust of the land became lice throughout all the land of Egypt. And the magicians did so with their enchantments to bring forth lice, but they could not: so there were lice upon man, and upon beast. Then the magicians said unto Pharaoh, This is the finger of God: and Pharaoh's heart was hardened, and he hearkened not unto them; as the Lord had said.

Exodus 8:16-19

But if I with the finger of God cast out devils, no doubt the kingdom of God is come upon you.

Luke 11:20

Rely upon the power of Jesus' name

Wherefore God also hath highly exalted him, and given him a name which is above every name: that at the name of Jesus every

52

knee should bow, of things in heaven, and things in earth, and things under the earth.

Philippians 2:9-10

Rely on the blood of the Lamb and the word of your testimony

And they overcame him by the blood of the Lamb, and by the word of their testimony; and they loved not their lives unto the death.

Revelation 12:11

Seek peace for your city

And seek the peace of the city whither I have caused you to be carried away captives, and pray unto the Lord for it: for in the peace thereof shall ye have peace.

Jeremiah 29:7

God will be an enemy to your enemies

But if thou shalt indeed obey his voice, and do all that I speak; then I will be an enemy unto thine enemies, and an adversary unto thine adversaries.

Exodus 23:22

Your mission is to turn people from the power of Satan unto God

To open their eyes, and to turn them from darkness to light, and from the power of Satan unto God, that they may receive forgiveness of sins, and inheritance among them which are sanctified by faith that is in me.

Acts 26:18

III. Steps for Deliverance

Begin the battle by praise and worship

And they rose early in the morning, and went forth into the wilderness of Tekoa: and as they went forth, Jehoshaphat stood and said, Hear me, O Judah, and ye inhabitants of Jerusalem; Believe in the Lord your God, so shall ye be established; believe his prophets, so shall ye prosper. And when he had consulted with the people, he appointed singers unto the Lord, and that should praise the beauty of holiness, as they went out before the army, and to say, Praise the Lord; for his mercy endureth for ever.

And when they began to sing and to praise, the Lord set ambushments against the children of Ammon, Moab, and mount Seir, which were come against Judah; and they were smitten.

2 Chronicles 20:20-22

Resist the devil

Be sober, be vigilant; because your adversary the devil, as a roaring lion, walketh about, seeking whom he may devour: whom resist stedfast in the faith, knowing that the same afflictions are accomplished in your brethren that are in the world.

1 Peter 5:8-9

Confess any sins

If we confess our sins, he is faithful and just to forgive us our sins, and to cleanse us from all unrighteousness.

1 John 1:9

Forgive anyone who may have wronged you

To whom ye forgive any thing, I forgive also: for if I forgave any thing, to whom I forgave it, for your sakes forgave I it in the person of Christ; lest Satan should get an advantage of us: for we are not ignorant of his devices.

2 Corinthians 2:10-11

Renounce any hidden things

But have renounced the hidden things of dishonesty, not walking in craftiness, nor handling the word of God deceitfully; but by manifestation of the truth commending ourselves to every man's conscience in the sight of God.

2 Corinthians 4:2

Have persistent faith in the Lord

And, behold, a woman of Canaan came out of the same coasts, and cried unto him, saying, Have mercy on me, O Lord, thou son of David; my daughter is grievously vexed with a devil. But he answered her not a word. And his disciples came and besought him, saying, Send her away; for she crieth after us. But he answered and said, I am not sent but unto the lost sheep of the house of Israel. Then came she and worshipped him, saying, Lord, help me. But he answered and said, It is not meet to take

the children's bread, and to cast it to dogs.
And she said, Truth, Lord: yet the dogs eat
of the crumbs which fall from their masters'
table. Then Jesus answered and said unto
her, O woman, great is thy faith: be it unto
thee even as thou wilt. And her daughter
was made whole from that very hour.

Matthew 15:22-28

Command the demons to leave

But he giveth more grace. Wherefore he
saith, God resisteth the proud, but giveth
grace unto the humble. Submit yourselves
therefore to God. Resist the devil, and he
will flee from you.

James 4:6-7

Use the authority of Jesus' name

And these signs shall follow them that
believe; In my name shall they cast out
devils; they shall speak with new tongues.

Mark 16:17

Recognize that the demons are already defeated

And the seventy returned again with joy,
saying, Lord, even the devils are subject

unto us through thy name. And he said unto them, I beheld Satan as lightning fall from heaven. Behold, I give unto you power to tread on serpents and scorpions, and over all the power of the enemy: and nothing shall by any means hurt you.

Luke 10:17-19

We are more than conquerors through him that loved us.

Romans 8:37

Accept the authority that Jesus gives His disciples

Then he called his twelve disciples together, and gave them power and authority over all devils, and to cure diseases.

Luke 9:1

Claim the power of Jesus' blood and confess your testimony

And they overcame him by the blood of the Lamb, and by the word of their testimony; and they loved not their lives unto the death.

Revelation 12:11

Wrestle with the spirits

For we wrestle not against flesh and blood, but against principalities, against powers, against the rulers of the darkness of this world, against spiritual wickedness in high places.

Ephesians 6:12

Tear down the strongholds

For though we walk in the flesh, we do not war after the flesh: (for the weapons of our warfare are not carnal, but mighty through God to the pulling down of strong holds;) casting down imaginations, and every high thing that exalteth itself against the knowledge of God, and bringing into captivity every thought to the obedience of Christ; and having in a readiness to revenge all disobedience, when your obedience is fulfilled.

2 Corinthians 10:3-6

Bind the spirits

Verily I say unto you, Whatsoever ye shall bind on earth shall be bound in heaven: and whatsoever ye shall loose on earth shall be loosed in heaven.

Matthew 18:18

Sometimes fasting is needed

And when he was come into the house, his disciples asked him privately, Why could not we cast him out? And he said unto them, This kind can come forth by nothing, but by prayer and fasting.

Mark 9:28-29

Sometimes prayer cloths are effective

And God wrought special miracles by the hands of Paul: so that from his body were brought unto the sick handkerchiefs or aprons, and the diseases departed from them, and the evil spirits went out of them.

Acts 19:11-12

Warn the one who is delivered that demons return to a house that makes them welcome

When the unclean spirit is gone out of a man, he walketh through dry places, seeking rest, and findeth none. Then he saith, I will return into my house from whence I came out; and when he is come, he findeth it empty, swept, and garnished. Then goeth he, and taketh with himself seven other spirits more wicked than himself, and they enter in and dwell there: and the last state of that man is worse than the first.

Matthew 12:43-45

Do not interfere with others casting out demons

And John answered him, saying, Master, we saw one casting out devils in thy name, and he followeth not us: and we forbad him, because he followeth not us. But Jesus said, Forbid him not: for there is no man which shall do a miracle in my name, that can lightly speak evil of me. For he that is not against us is on our part.

Mark 9:38-40

PART THREE

Know That Angels Are Involved in Defeating the Enemy

I. What the Scriptures Teach About Obtaining the Help of Angels

Angels obey God's commands about everything, including protecting and meeting the needs of the heirs of salvation

Because thou hast made the Lord, which is my refuge, even the most High, thy habitation; there shall no evil befall thee, neither shall any plague come nigh thy dwelling. For he shall give his angels charge over thee, to keep thee in all thy ways. They shall bear thee up in their hands, lest thou dash thy foot against a stone. Thou shalt tread upon the lion and adder: the

young lion and the dragon shalt thou
trample under feet.

Psalm 91:9-13

Bless the Lord, ye his angels, that excel in
strength, that do his commandments,
hearkening unto the voice of his word.
Bless ye the Lord, all ye his hosts; ye
ministers of his, that do his pleasure.

Psalm 103:20-21

Are they not all ministering spirits, sent
forth to minister for them who shall be
heirs of salvation?

Hebrews 1:14

The Lord's angels surround those who fear God to deliver them

The angel of the Lord encampeth round
about them that fear him, and delivereth
them.

Psalm 34:7

And when the servant of the man of God
was risen early, and gone forth, behold, an
host compassed the city both with horses
and chariots. And his servants said unto
him, Alas, my master! how shall we do?

64

And he answered, Fear not: for they that be with us are more than they that be with them. And Elisha prayed, and said, Lord, I pray thee, open his eyes, that he may see. And the Lord opened the eyes of the young man; and he saw: and, behold, the mountain was full of horses and chariots of fire round about Elisha.

2 Kings 6:15-17

The Lord's angels engage in combat against the devil's angels

And there was war in heaven: Michael and his angels fought against the dragon; and the dragon fought and his angels, and prevailed not; neither was their place found any more in heaven. And the great dragon was cast out, that old serpent, called the Devil, and Satan, which deceiveth the whole world: he was cast out into the earth, and his angels were cast out with him.

Revelation 12:7-9

Prayer is recorded which requested the assistance of angels

Plead my cause, O Lord, with them that strive with me: fight against them that fight against me. Take hold of shield and buckler, and stand up for mine help. Draw out also the spear, and stop the way against them that persecute me: say unto my soul, I am thy salvation. Let them be confounded and put to shame that seek after my soul: let them be turned back and brought to confusion that devise my hurt. Let them be as chaff before the wind: and let the angel of the Lord chase them. Let their way be dark and slippery: and let the angel of the Lord persecute them.

Psalm 35:1-6

Jesus said that He could pray to the Father and call more than twelve legions of angels

Thinkest thou that I cannot now pray to my Father, and he shall presently give me more than twelve legions of angels?

Matthew 26:53

Angels are sent in answer to prayer

And for this cause Hezekiah the king, and the prophet Isaiah the son of Amoz, prayed and cried to heaven.

And the Lord sent an angel, which cut off all the mighty men of valour, and the leaders and captains in the camp of the king of Assyria. So he returned with shame of face to his own land. And when he was come into the house of his god, they that came forth of his own bowels slew him there with the sword.

2 Chronicles 32:20-21

Peter therefore was kept in prison. but prayer was made without ceasing of the church unto God for him. And when Herod would have brought him forth, the same night Peter was sleeping between two soldiers, bound with two chains: and the keepers before the door kept the prison. And, behold, the angel of the Lord came upon him, and a light shined in the prison: and he smote Peter on the side, and raised him up, saying, Arise up quickly. And his chains fell off from his hands.

Acts 12:5-7

Angels can give strength to humans

Then there came again and touched me one like the appearance of a man, and he strengthened me, and said, O man greatly beloved, fear not: peace be unto thee, be strong, yea, be strong. And when he had spoken unto me, I was strengthened, and said, Let my lord speak; for thou hast strengthened me.

Daniel 10:18-19

Angels will be judged (being rewarded for their effectiveness) by the believers whom the angels were assigned to assist

Know ye not that we shall judge angels? how much more things that pertain to this life?

1 Corinthians 6:3

We are not to worship angels

Let no man beguile you of your reward in a voluntary humility and worshipping of angels, intruding into those things which he hath not seen, vainly puffed up by his fleshly mind, and not holding the Head, from which all the body by joints and

68

bands having nourishment ministered, and knit together, increaseth with the increase of God.

Colossians 2:18-19

And I John saw these things, and heard them. And when I had heard and seen, I fell down to worship before the feet of the angel which shewed me these things. Then he said unto me, See thou do it not: for I am thy fellowservant, and of thy brethren the prophets, and of them which keep the sayings of this book: worship God.

Revelation 22:8-9

II. What the Scriptures Say About the Origin of Angels

Angels were created by the Lord

Praise ye him, all his angels: praise ye him, all his hosts. Praise ye him, sun and moon: praise him, all ye stars of light. Praise him, ye heavens of heavens, and ye waters that be above the heavens. Let them praise the name of the Lord: for he commanded, and they were created.

Psalm 148:2-5

For by him were all things created, that are in heaven, and that are in earth, visible and invisible, whether they be thrones, or dominions, or principalities, or powers: all things were created by him, and for him: and he is before all things, and by him all things consist.

Colossians 1:16-17

Angels are spirit-beings

And of the angels he saith, Who maketh his angels spirits, and his ministers a flame of fire.

Hebrews 1:7

Angels were present when the earth was created

Where wast thou when I laid the foundations of the earth? declare, if thou hast understanding....When the morning stars sang together, and all the sons of God shouted for joy?

Job 38:4,7

Angels number into many multitudes

The chariots of God are twenty thousand, even thousands of angels: the Lord is among them, as in Sinai, in the holy place.

Psalm 68:17

And I beheld, and I heard the voice of many angels round about the throne and the beasts and the elders: and the number of them was ten thousand times ten thousand, and thousands of thousands.

Revelation 5:11

III. What the Scriptures Say About Angels' Characteristics and Activities

Angels are mighty

Bless the Lord, ye his angels, that excel in strength, that do his commandments, hearkening unto the voice of his word.

Psalm 103:20

Whereas angels, which are greater in power and might, bring not railing accusation against them before the Lord.

2 Peter 2:11

Angels are holy

When the Son of man shall come in his glory, and all the holy angels with him, then shall he sit upon the throne of his glory.

Matthew 25:31

And they said, Cornelius the centurion, a just man, and one that feareth God, and of good report among all the nation of the Jews, was warned from God by an holy angel to send for thee into his house, and to hear words of thee.

Acts 10:22

Angels behold the face of God

Take heed that ye despise not one of these little ones; for I say unto you, That in heaven their angels do always behold the face of my Father which is in heaven.

Matthew 18:10

Likewise, I say unto you, there is joy in the presence of the angels of God over one sinner that repenteth.

Luke 15:10

Angels praise the Lord

Praise ye the Lord. Praise ye the Lord from the heavens: praise him in the heights. Praise ye him, all his angels: praise ye him, all his hosts.

Psalm 148:1-2

And suddenly there was with the angel a multitude of the heavenly host praising God, and saying, Glory to God in the highest, and on earth peace, good will toward men.

Luke 2:13-14

And again, when he bringeth in the first begotten into the world, he saith, And let all the angels of God worship him.

Hebrews 1:6

And I beheld, and I heard the voice of many angels round about the throne and the beasts and the elders: and the number of them was ten thousand times ten thousand, and thousands of thousands; saying with a loud voice, Worthy is the Lamb that was slain to receive power, and riches, and

73

wisdom, and strength, and honour, and
glory, and blessing.

Revelation 5:11-12

And all the angels stood round about the
throne, and about the elders and the four
beasts, and fell before the throne on their
faces, and worshipped God, saying, Amen:
Blessing, and glory, and wisdom, and
thanksgiving, and honour, and power, and
might, be unto our God for ever and ever.
Amen.

Revelation 7:11-12

**Angels were involved in carrying the
righteous to heaven**

And it came to pass, as they still went on,
and talked, that, behold, there appeared a
chariot of fire, and horses of fire, and
parted them both asunder; and Elijah went
up by a whirlwind into heaven.

2 Kings 2:11

There was a certain rich man, which was
clothed in purple and fine linen, and fared
sumptuously every day: and there was a
certain beggar named Lazarus, which was
laid at his gate, full of sores, and desiring to

be fed with the crumbs which fell from the rich man's table: moreover the dogs came and licked his sores. And it came to pass, that the beggar died, and was carried by the angels into Abraham's bosom: the rich man also died, and was buried.

Luke 16:19-22

Angels do not marry and do not die

For when they shall rise from the dead, they neither marry, nor are given in marriage; but are as the angels which are in heaven.

Mark 12:25

And Jesus answering said unto them, The children of this world marry, and are given in marriage: but they which shall be accounted worthy to obtain that world, and the resurrection from the dead, neither marry, nor are given in marriage: neither can they die any more: for they are equal unto the angels; and are the children of God, being the children of the resurrection.

Luke 20:34-36

Angels, though intelligent, are limited in their knowledge

But of that day and hour knoweth no man, no, not the angels of heaven, but my Father only.

Matthew 24:36

Unto whom it was revealed, that not unto themselves, but unto us they did minister the things, which are now reported unto you by them that have preached the gospel unto you with the Holy Ghost sent down from heaven; which things the angels desire to look into.

1 Peter 1:12

Angels are limited in scope

For unto the angels hath he not put in subjection the world to come, whereof we speak.

Hebrews 2:5

Angels eat manna

Though he had commanded the clouds from above, and opened the doors of heaven, and had rained down manna upon them to eat, and had given them of the

76

corn of heaven. Man did eat angels' food:
he sent them meat to the full.

Psalm 78:23-25

When Christ returns to earth, angels will accompany Him and will gather His elect

For the Son of man shall come in the
glory of his Father with his angels; and then
he shall reward every man according to his
works.

Matthew 16:27

And he shall send his angels with a great
sound of a trumpet, and they shall gather
together his elect from the four winds, from
one end of heaven to the other.

Matthew 24:31

Whosoever therefore shall be ashamed of
me and of my words in this adulterous and
sinful generation; of him also shall the Son
of man be ashamed, when he cometh in the
glory of his Father with the holy angels.

Mark 8:38

And then shall he send his angels, and
shall gather together his elect from the four

winds, from the uttermost part of the earth to the uttermost part of heaven.

Mark 13:27

For whosoever shall be ashamed of me and of my words, of him shall the Son of man be ashamed, when he shall come in his own glory, and in his Father's, and of the holy angels.

Luke 9:26

Also I say unto you, Whosoever shall confess me before men, him shall the Son of man also confess before the angels of God: but he that denieth me before men shall be denied before the angels of God.

Luke 12:8-9

Angels will assist in carrying out the Lord's vengeance on those who do not know God

Then Jesus sent the multitude away, and went into the house: and his disciples came unto him, saying, Declare unto us the parable of the tares of the field. He answered and said unto them, He that soweth the good seed is the Son of man; the field is the world; the good seed are the

children of the kingdom; but the tares are
the children of the wicked one; the enemy
that sowed them is the devil; the harvest is
the end of the world; and the reapers are
the angels. As therefore the tares are
gathered and burned in the fire; so shall it
be in the end of this world. The Son of
man shall send forth his angels, and they
shall gather out of his kingdom all things
that offend, and them which do iniquity;
and shall cast them into a furnace of fire:
there shall be wailing and gnashing of teeth.
Matthew 13:36-42

Again, the kingdom of heaven is like unto
a net, that was cast into the sea, and
gathered of every kind: which, when it was
full, they drew to shore, and sat down, and
gathered the good into vessels, but cast the
bad away. So shall it be at the end of the
world: the angels shall come forth, and
sever the wicked from among the just, and
shall cast them into the furnace of fire:
there shall be wailing and gnashing of teeth.
Matthew 13:47-50

And to you who are troubled rest with
us, when the Lord Jesus shall be revealed

from heaven with his mighty angels, in flaming fire taking vengeance on them that know not God, and that obey not the gospel of our Lord Jesus Christ.

2 Thessalonians 1:7-9

An angel will bind Satan and put him into the bottomless pit

And I saw an angel come down from heaven, having the key of the bottomless pit and a great chain in his hand. And he laid hold on the dragon, that old serpent, which is the Devil, and Satan, and bound him a thousand years, and cast him into the bottomless pit, and shut him up, and set a seal upon him, that he should deceive the nations no more, till the thousand years should be fulfilled: and after that he must be loosed a little season.

Revelation 20:1-3

IV. What the Scriptures Say About the Appearance of Angels

Some angels have the appearance of men

And there came two angels to Sodom at even; and Lot sat in the gate of Sodom: and Lot seeing them rose up to meet them; and he bowed himself with his face toward the ground; and he said, Behold now, my lords, turn in, I pray you, into your servant's house, and tarry all night, and wash your feet, and ye shall rise up early, and go on your ways. And they said, Nay; but we will abide in the street all night. And he pressed upon them greatly; and they turned in unto him, and entered into his house; and he made them a feast, and did bake unleavened bread, and they did eat.

Genesis 19:1-3

And Jacob was left alone; and there wrestled a man with him until the breaking of the day. And when he saw that he prevailed not against him, he touched the hollow of his thigh; and the hollow of

Jacob's thigh was out of joint, as he wrestled with him. And he said, Let me go, for the day breaketh. And he said, I will not let thee go, except thou bless me. And he said unto him, What is thy name? And he said, Jacob. And he said, Thy name shall be called no more Jacob, but Israel: for as a prince hast thou power with God and with men, and hast prevailed. And Jacob asked him, and said, Tell me, I pray thee, thy name. And he said, Wherefore is it that thou dost ask after my name? And he blessed him there.

Genesis 32:24-29

Then the woman came and told her husband, saying, A man of God came unto me, and his countenance was like the countenance of an angel of God, very terrible: but I asked him not whence he was, neither told he me his name.

Judges 13:6

And it came to pass, when I, even I Daniel, had seen the vision, and sought for the meaning, then, behold, there stood before me as the appearance of a man. And I heard a man's voice between the banks of

Ulai, which called, and said, Gabriel, make this man to understand the vision. So he came near where I stood: and when he came, I was afraid, and fell upon my face: but he said unto me, Understand, O son of man: for at the time of the end shall be the vision. Now as he was speaking with me, I was in a deep sleep on my face toward the ground: but he touched me, and set me upright. And he said, Behold, I will make thee know what shall be in the last end of the indignation: for at the time appointed the end shall be.

Daniel 8:15-19

Then I lifted up mine eyes, and looked, and behold a certain man clothed in linen, whose loins were girded with fine gold of Uphaz: his body also was like the beryl, and his face as the appearance of lightning, and his eyes as lamps of fire, and his arms and his feet like in colour to polished brass, and the voice of his words like the voice of a multitude.

Daniel 10:5-6

Then there came again and touched me
one like the appearance of a man, and he
strengthened me.

Daniel 10:18

In the end of the sabbath, as it began to
dawn toward the first day of the week,
came Mary Magdalene and the other Mary
to see the sepulchre. And, behold, there
was a great earthquake: for the angel of the
Lord descended from heaven, and came and
rolled back the stone from the door, and sat
upon it. His countenance was like lightning,
and his raiment white as snow.

Matthew 28:1-3

And when they looked, they saw that the
stone was rolled away: for it was very
great. And entering into the sepulchre, they
saw a young man sitting on the right side,
clothed in a long white garment; and they
were affrighted. And he saith unto them, Be
not affrighted: Ye seek Jesus of Nazareth,
which was crucified: he is risen; he is not
here: behold the place where they laid him.
But go your way, tell his disciples and Peter

that he goeth before you into Galilee: there
shall ye see him, as he said unto you.

Mark 16:4-7

And they entered in, and found not the
body of the Lord Jesus. And it came to pass,
as they were much perplexed thereabout,
behold, two men stood by them in shining
garments: and as they were afraid, and
bowed down their faces to the earth, they
said unto them, Why seek ye the living
among the dead? He is not here, but is
risen: remember how he spake unto you
when he was yet in Galilee, saying, The Son
of man must be delivered into the hands of
sinful men, and be crucified, and the third
day rise again.

Luke 24:3-7

And when he had spoken these things,
while they beheld, he was taken up; and a
cloud received him out of their sight. And
while they looked stedfastly toward heaven
as he went up, behold, two men stood by
them in white apparel; which also said, Ye
men of Galilee, why stand ye gazing up into
heaven? this same Jesus, which is taken up
from you into heaven, shall so come in like

manner as ye have seen him go into heaven.

Acts 1:9-11

And laid their hands on the apostles, and put them in the common prison. But the angel of the Lord by night opened the prison doors, and brought them forth, and said, Go, stand and speak in the temple to the people all the words of this life.

Acts 5:18-20

Some angels are multi-winged

In the year that king Uzziah died I saw also the Lord sitting upon a throne, high and lifted up, and his train filled the temple. Above it stood the seraphims: each one had six wings; with twain he covered his face, and with twain he covered his feet, and with twain he did fly. And one cried unto another, and said, Holy, holy, holy, is the Lord of hosts: the whole earth is full of his glory.

Isaiah 6:1-3

Some angels are multi-faced

Also out of the midst thereof came the likeness of four living creatures. And this

86

was their appearance; they had the likeness
of a man. And every one had four faces,
and every one had four wings. And their
feet were straight feet; and the sole of their
feet was like the sole of a calf's foot; and
they sparkled like the colour of burnished
brass. And they had the hands of a man
under their wings on their four sides; and
they four had their faces and their wings.
Their wings were joined one to another;
they turned not when they went; they went
every one straight forward. As for the
likeness of their faces, they four had the
face of a man, and the face of a lion, on the
right side: and they four had the face of an
ox on the left side; they four also had the
face of an eagle. Thus were their faces: and
their wings were stretched upward; two
wings of every one were joined one to
another, and two covered their bodies. And
they went every one straight forward:
whither the spirit was to go, they went;
and they turned not when they went. As
for the likeness of the living creatures, their
appearance was like burning coals of fire,
and like the appearance of lamps; it went
up and down among the living creatures;
and the fire was bright, and out of the fire

went forth lightning. And the living creatures ran and returned as the appearance of a flash of lightning.

Ezekiel 1:5-14

And I saw as the colour of amber, as the appearance of fire round about within it, from the appearance of his loins even upward, and from the appearance of his loins even downward, I saw as it were the appearance of fire, and it had brightness round about. As the appearance of the bow that is in the cloud of the day of rain, so was the appearance of the brightness round about. This was the appearance of the likeness of the glory of the Lord. And when I saw it, I fell upon my face, and I heard a voice of one that spake.

Ezekiel 1:27-28

Then I looked, and, behold, in the firmament that was above the head of the cherubims there appeared over them as it were a sapphire stone, as the appearance of the likeness of a throne. And he spake unto the man clothed with linen, and said, Go in between the wheels, even under the cherub, and fill thine hand with coals of fire from between the cherubims, and scatter them over the city. And he went in in my sight. Now the cherubims stood on the right side of the house, when the man went in; and the cloud filled the inner court. Then the glory of the Lord went up from the cherub, and stood over the threshold of the house; and the house was filled with the cloud, and the court was full of the brightness of the Lord's glory. And the sound of the cherubims' wings was heard even to the outer court, as the voice of the Almighty God when he speaketh. And it came to pass, that when he had commanded the man clothed with linen, saying, Take fire from between the wheels, from between the cherubims; then he went in, and stood beside the wheels. And one cherub stretched forth his hand from between the cherubims unto the fire that was between the cherubims, and took thereof, and put it into the hands of him that was clothed with linen: who took it, and went out.

And there appeared in the cherubims the form of a man's hand under their wings. And when I looked, behold the four wheels by the cherubims, one wheel by one cherub, and another wheel by another

cherub: and the appearance of the wheels
was as the colour of a beryl stone. And as
for their appearances, they four had one
likeness as if a wheel had been in the midst
of a wheel. When they went, they went
upon their four sides; they turned not as
they went, but to the place whither the
head looked they followed it; they turned
not as they went. And their whole body,
and their backs, and their hands, and their
wings, and the wheels, were full of eyes
round about, even the wheels that they four
had. As for the wheels, it was cried unto
them in my hearing, O wheel. And every
one had four faces: the first face was the
face of a cherub, and the second face was
the face of a man, and the third the face of
a lion, and the fourth the face of an eagle.
And the cherubims were lifted up. This is
the living creature that I saw by the river of
Chebar. And when the cherubims went, the
wheels went by them: and when the
cherubims lifted up their wings to mount
up from the earth, the same wheels also
turned not from beside them. When they
stood, these stood; and when they were
lifted up, these lifted up themselves also:
for the spirit of the living creature was in

them. Then the glory of the Lord departed from off the threshold of the house, and stood over the cherubims. And the cherubims lifted up their wings, and mounted up from the earth in my sight: when they went out, the wheels also were beside them, and every one stood at the door of the east gate of the Lord's house; and the glory of the God of Israel was over them above. This is the living creature that I saw under the God of Israel by the river of Chebar; and I knew that they were the cherubims. Every one had four faces apiece, and every one four wings; and the likeness of the hands of a man was under their wings. And the likeness of their faces was the same faces which I saw by the river of Chebar, their appearances and themselves: they went every one straight forward.

Ezekiel 10:1-22

Some angels have the appearance of fire

Then I beheld, and lo a likeness as the appearance of fire: from the appearance of his loins even downward, fire; and from his loins even upward, as the appearance of brightness, as the colour of amber.

Ezekiel 8:2

Some spirit-beings have the appearance of horses

I saw by night, and behold a man riding upon a red horse, and he stood among the myrtle trees that were in the bottom; and behind him were there red horses, speckled, and white. Then said I, O my lord, what are these? and the angel that talked with me said unto me, I will shew thee what these be. And the man that stood among the myrtle trees answered and said, These are they whom the Lord hath sent to walk to and fro through the earth. And they answered the angel of the Lord that stood among the myrtle trees, and said, We have walked to and fro through the earth, and, behold, all the earth sitteth still, and is at rest.

Zechariah 1:8-11

And I turned, and lifted up mine eyes, and looked, and, behold, there came four chariots out from between two mountains; and the mountains were mountains of brass.

In the first chariot were red horses; and in the second chariot black horses; and in the third chariot white horses; and in the fourth chariot grisled and bay horses. Then I answered and said unto the angel that talked with me, What are these, my lord. And the angel answered and said unto me, These are the four spirits of the heavens, which go forth from standing before the Lord of all the earth. The black horses which are therein go forth into the north country; and the white go forth after them; and the grisled go forth toward the south country. And the bay went forth, and sought to go that they might walk to and fro through the earth: and he said, Get you hence, walk to and fro through the earth. So they walked to and fro through the earth. Then cried he upon me, and spake unto me, saying, Behold, these that go toward the north country have quieted my spirit in the north country.

Zechariah 6:1-8

And I saw heaven opened, and behold a white horse; and he that sat upon him was called Faithful and True, and in righteousness he doth judge and make war. His eyes

were as a flame of fire, and on his head
were many crowns; and he had a name
written, that no man knew, but he himself.
And he was clothed with a vesture dipped
in blood: and his name is called The Word
of God. And the armies which were in
heaven followed him upon white horses,
clothed in fine linen, white and clean.

Revelation 19:11-14

Some spirit-beings have the faces of beasts

And before the throne there was a sea of
glass like unto crystal: and in the midst of
the throne, and round about the throne,
were four beasts full of eyes before and
behind. And the first beast was like a lion,
and the second beast like a calf, and the
third beast had a face as a man, and the
fourth beast was like a flying eagle. And the
four beasts had each of them six wings
about him; and they were full of eyes
within: and they rest not day and night,
saying, Holy, holy, holy, Lord God
Almighty, which was, and is, and is
to come.

Revelation 4:6-8

V. What the Scriptures Say About the Titles of Angels

Angels have names

Gabriel

And I heard a man's voice between the banks of Ulai, which called, and said, Gabriel, make this man to understand the vision.

Daniel 8:16

And the angel answering said unto him, I am Gabriel, that stand in the presence of God; and am sent to speak unto thee, and to shew thee these glad tidings.

Luke 1:19

Michael

But the prince of the kingdom of Persia withstood me one and twenty days: but, lo, Michael, one of the chief princes, came to help me; and I remained there with the kings of Persia.

Daniel 10:13

Some angel names may be beyond our understanding

And the angel of the Lord said unto him, Why askest thou thus after my name, seeing it is secret?

Judges 13:18

"It is beyond understanding" (NIV)
"Wonderful" (NASB)

Angels have titles indicating rank

Cherubim

So he drove out the man; and he placed at the east of the garden of Eden Cherubims, and a flaming sword which turned every way, to keep the way of the tree of life.

Genesis 3:24

Seraphim

In the year that king Uzziah died I saw also the Lord sitting upon a throne, high and lifted up, and his train filled the temple. Above it stood the seraphims: each one had six wings; with twain he covered his

face, and with twain he covered his feet,
and with twain he did fly.

Isaiah 6:1-2

Chief Prince

But the prince of the kingdom of Persia
withstood me one and twenty days: but, lo,
Michael, one of the chief princes, came to
help me; and I remained there with the
kings of Persia.

Daniel 10:13

Great Prince

And at that time shall Michael stand up,
the great prince which standeth for the
children of thy people: and there shall be a
time of trouble, such as never was since
there was a nation even to that same time:
and at that time thy people shall be
delivered, every one that shall be found
written in the book.

Daniel 12:1

Your Prince

But I will shew thee that which is noted
in the scripture of truth: and there is none

that holdeth with me in these things, but Michael your prince.

Daniel 10:21

Archangel

Yet Michael the archangel, when contending with the devil he disputed about the body of Moses, durst not bring against him a railing accusation, but said, The Lord rebuke thee.

Jude 9

Strong Angel

And I saw a strong angel proclaiming with a loud voice, Who is worthy to open the book, and to loose the seals thereof?

Revelation 5:2

Mighty Angel

And I saw another mighty angel come down from heaven, clothed with a cloud: and a rainbow was upon his head, and his face was as it were the sun, and his feet as pillars of fire.

Revelation 10:1

And a mighty angel took up a stone like a great millstone, and cast it into the sea, saying, Thus with violence shall that great city Babylon be thrown down, and shall be found no more at all.

Revelation 18:21

VI. What the Old Testament Says About the Activity of Angels in Human Lives

Angels guarded the tree of life

So he drove out the man; and he placed at the east of the garden of Eden Cherubims, and a flaming sword which turned every way, to keep the way of the tree of life.

Genesis 3:24

An angel named Hagar's son and delivered God's promise about him

But Abram said unto Sarai, Behold, thy maid is in thy hand; do to her as it pleaseth thee. And when Sarai dealt hardly with her, she fled from her face.

And the angel of the Lord found her by a

fountain of water in the wilderness, by the fountain in the way to Shur. And he said, Hagar, Sarai's maid, whence camest thou? and whither wilt thou go? And she said, I flee from the face of my mistress Sarai. And the angel of the Lord said unto her, Return to thy mistress, and submit thyself under her hands. And the angel of the Lord said unto her, I will multiply thy seed exceedingly, that it shall not be numbered for multitude. And the angel of the Lord said unto her, Behold, thou art with child, and shalt bear a son, and shalt call his name Ishmael; because the Lord hath heard thy affliction. And he will be a wild man; his hand will be against every man, and every man's hand against him; and he shall dwell in the presence of all his brethren.

Genesis 16:6-12

Two angels visited Lot and rescued him from the homosexuals of Sodom by blinding the men

And there came two angels to Sodom at even; and Lot sat in the gate of Sodom: and Lot seeing them rose up to meet them; and he bowed himself with his face toward the ground; and he said, Behold now, my lords, turn in, I pray you, into your servant's house, and tarry all night, and wash your feet, and ye shall rise up early, and go on your ways. And they said, Nay; but we will abide in the street all night. And he pressed upon them greatly; and they turned in unto him, and entered into his house; and he made them a feast, and did bake unleavened bread, and they did eat.

But before they lay down, the men of the city, even the men of Sodom, compassed the house round, both old and young, all the people from every quarter: and they called unto Lot, and said unto him, Where are the men which came in to thee this night? bring them out unto us, that we may know them. And Lot went out at the door unto them, and shut the door after him, and said, I pray you, brethren, do not so wickedly. Behold now, I have two daughters which have not known man; let me, I pray you, bring them out unto you, and do ye to them as is good in your eyes: only unto these men do nothing; for therefore came they under the shadow of my roof. And they said, Stand back. And they said again, This one fellow came in to sojourn, and he will needs be a judge: now will we deal worse with thee, than with them. And they pressed sore upon the man, even Lot, and came near to break the door. But the men put forth their hand, and pulled Lot into the house to them, and shut to the door. And they smote the men that were at the door of the house with blindness, both small and great: so that they wearied themselves to find the door.

Genesis 19:1-11

Two angels warned Lot to save his family, granted permission for him to escape to Zoar, then destroyed Sodom and Gomorrah

And the men said unto Lot, Hast thou here any besides? son-in-law, and thy sons, and thy daughters, and whatsoever thou hast in the city, bring them out of this place: for we will destroy this place, because the cry of them is waxen great before the face of the Lord; and the Lord hath sent us to destroy it. And Lot went out, and spake unto his sons in law, which married his daughters, and said, Up, get you out of this place; for the Lord will destroy this city. But he seemed as one that mocked unto his sons in law.

Genesis 19:12-14

An angel assured Hagar that God would make Ishmael a great nation

And Abraham rose up early in the morning, and took bread, and a bottle of water, and gave it unto Hagar, putting it on her shoulder, and the child, and sent her away: and she departed, and wandered in the wilderness of Beersheba. And the water was spent in the bottle, and she cast the child under one of the shrubs. And she went, and sat her down over against him a good way off, as it were a bowshot: for she said, Let me not see the death of the child. And she sat over against him, and lift up her voice, and wept. And God heard the voice of the lad; and the angel of God called to Hagar out of heaven, and said unto her, What aileth thee, Hagar? fear not; for God hath heard the voice of the lad where he is. Arise, lift up the lad, and hold him in thine hand; for I will make him a great nation.

Genesis 21:14-18

An angel brought God's words to Abraham, sparing the life of Isaac

And Isaac spake unto Abraham his father, and said, My father: and he said, Here am I, my son. And he said, Behold the fire and the wood: but where is the lamb for a burnt offering? And Abraham said, My son, God will provide himself a lamb for a burnt offering: so they went both of them together. And they came to the place which God had told him of; and Abraham built an altar there, and laid the wood in order, and bound Isaac his son, and laid him on the altar upon the wood. And Abraham stretched forth his hand, and took the knife to slay his son. And the angel of the Lord called unto him out of heaven, and said, Abraham, Abraham: and he said, Here am I. And he said, Lay not thine hand upon the lad, neither do thou any thing unto him; for now I know that thou fearest God, seeing thou hast not withheld thy son, thine only son from me. And Abraham lifted up his eyes, and looked, and behold behind him a ram caught in a thicket by his horns: and Abraham went and took the ram, and offered him up for a burnt offering in the stead of his son.

Genesis 22:7-13

Angels appeared in Jacob's dream at Bethel

And he lighted upon a certain place, and tarried there all night, because the sun was set; and he took of the stones of that place, and put them for his pillows, and lay down in that place to sleep. And he dreamed, and behold a ladder set up on the earth, and the top of it reached to heaven: and behold the angels of God ascending and descending on it.

Genesis 28:11-12

Angels instructed Jacob in a dream to return to Canaan

And the angel of God spake unto me in a dream, saying, Jacob: And I said, Here am I. And he said, Lift up now thine eyes, and see, all the rams which leap upon the cattle are ringstraked, speckled, and grisled: for I have seen all that Laban doeth unto thee. I am the God of Bethel, where thou anointedst the pillar, and where thou

vowedst a vow unto me: now arise, get
thee out from this land, and return unto the
land of thy kindred.

Genesis 31:11-13

Angels met Jacob as he journeyed homeward

And Jacob went on his way, and the
angels of God met him. And when Jacob
saw them, he said, This is God's host: and
he called the name of that place Mahanaim.

Genesis 32:1-2

An angel wrestled with Jacob, disjointed his thigh, named him Israel, and blessed him

And Jacob was left alone; and there
wrestled a man with him until the breaking
of the day. And when he saw that he
prevailed not against him, he touched the
hollow of his thigh; and the hollow of
Jacob's thigh was out of joint, as he
wrestled with him. And he said, Let me go,
for the day breaketh. And he said, I will not
let thee go, except thou bless me. And he
said unto him, What is thy name? And he
said, Jacob. And he said, Thy name shall be
called no more Jacob, but Israel: for as a

prince hast thou power with God and with men, and hast prevailed. And Jacob asked him, and said, Tell me, I pray thee, thy name. And he said, Wherefore is it that thou dost ask after my name? And he blessed him there.

Genesis 32:24-29

An angel appeared to Moses from a burning bush

Now Moses kept the flock of Jethro his father-in-law, the priest of Midian: and he led the flock to the backside of the desert, and came to the mountain of God, even to Horeb. And the angel of the Lord appeared unto him in a flame of fire out of the midst of a bush: and he looked, and, behold, the bush burned with fire, and the bush was not consumed. And Moses said, I will now turn aside, and see this great sight, why the bush is not burnt.

Exodus 3:1-3

An angel went before the Israelites when they were fleeing from Egypt, and he stood between them and their pursuers

And the angel of God, which went before the camp of Israel, removed and went behind them; and the pillar of the cloud went from before their face, and stood behind them.

Exodus 14:19

God instructed Israel to obey the angel He sent to guide and protect them

Behold, I send an Angel before thee, to keep thee in the way, and to bring thee into the place which I have prepared. Beware of him, and obey his voice, provoke him not; for he will not pardon your transgressions: for my name is in him. But if thou shalt indeed obey his voice, and do all that I speak; then I will be an enemy unto thine enemies, and an adversary unto thine adversaries. For mine Angel shall go before thee, and bring thee in unto the Amorites, and the Hittites, and the Perrizzites, and the Canaanites, the

Hivites, and the Jebusites: and I will cut them off.

Exodus 23:20-23

An angel withstood Balaam. Balaam's ass saw the angel, stopped and took a beating. Then God spoke through the ass and opened Balaam's eyes to see the angel with a drawn sword

And Balaam rose up in the morning, and saddled his ass, and went with the princes of Moab.

And God's anger was kindled because he went: and the angel of the Lord stood in the way for an adversary against him. Now he was riding upon his ass, and his two servants were with him. And the ass saw the angel of the Lord standing in the way, and his sword drawn in his hand: and the ass turned aside out of the way, and went into the field: and Balaam smote the ass, to turn her into the way. But the angel of the Lord stood in a path of the vineyards, a wall being on this side, and a wall on that side. And when the ass saw the angel of the Lord, she thrust herself unto the wall, and crushed Balaam's foot against the wall: and he smote her again. And the angel of the

Lord went further, and stood in a narrow place, where was no way to turn either to the right hand or to the left. And when the ass saw the angel of the Lord, she fell down under Balaam: and Balaam's anger was kindled, and he smote the ass with a staff. And the Lord opened the mouth of the ass, and she said unto Balaam, What have I done unto thee, that thou hast smitten me these three times? And Balaam said unto the ass, Because thou hast mocked me: I would there were a sword in mine hand, for now would I kill thee. And the ass said unto Balaam, Am not I thine ass, upon which thou hast ridden ever since I was thine unto this day? was I ever wont to do so unto thee? And he said, Nay. Then the Lord opened the eyes of Balaam, and he saw the angel of the Lord standing in the way, and his sword drawn in his hand: and he bowed down his head, and fell flat on his face. And the angel of the Lord said unto him, Wherefore hast thou smitten thine ass these three times? behold, I went out to withstand thee, because thy way is perverse before me: and the ass saw me, and turned from me these three times: unless she had turned from me, surely now also I had slain thee, and saved her alive. And Balaam said unto the angel of the Lord, I have sinned; for I knew not that thou stoodest in the way against me: now therefore, if it displease thee, I will get me back again. And the angel of the Lord said unto Balaam, Go with the men: but only the word that I shall speak unto thee, that thou shalt speak. So Balaam went with the princes of Balak.

Numbers 22:21-35

An angel warned the Israelites not to make a league with the inhabitants of Canaan and assured them that God would not break His covenant

And an angel of the Lord came up from Gilgal to Bochim, and said, I made you to go up out of Egypt, and have brought you unto the land which I sware unto your fathers; and I said, I will never break my covenant with you. And ye shall make no league with the inhabitants of this land; ye shall throw down their altars; but ye have not obeyed my voice: why have ye done this? Wherefore I also said, I will not drive them out from before you; but they shall be as thorns in your sides, and their gods shall be a snare unto you. And it came to pass, when the angel of the Lord spake these words unto all the children of Israel, that the people lifted up their voice, and wept. And they called the name of that place Bochim: and they sacrificed there unto the Lord.

Judges 2:1-5

An angel instructed that Meroz be cursed

Curse ye Meroz, said the angel of the Lord, curse ye bitterly the inhabitants thereof; because they came not to the help of the Lord, to the help of the Lord against the mighty.

Judges 5:23

An angel announced to Gideon that he was a man of valor

And there came an angel of the Lord, and sat under an oak which was in Ophrah, that pertained unto Joash the Abiezrite: and his son Gideon threshed wheat by the wine-press, to hide it from the Midianites. And the angel of the Lord appeared unto him, and said unto him, The Lord is with thee, thou mighty man of valour. And Gideon said unto him, Oh my Lord, if the Lord be with us, why then is all this befallen us? and where be all his miracles which our fathers told us of, saying, Did not the Lord bring us up from Egypt? but now the Lord hath forsaken us, and delivered us into the hands of the Midianites. And the Lord looked upon him, and said, Go in this thy might, and thou shalt save Israel from the hand of the Midianites: have not I sent thee? And he said unto him, Oh my Lord, wherewith shall I save Israel? behold, my family is poor in Manasseh, and I am the least in my father's house. And the Lord said unto him, Surely I will be with thee, and thou shalt smite the Midianites as one man. And he said unto him, If now I have found grace in thy sight, then shew me a sign that thou talkest with me. Depart not hence, I pray thee, until I come unto thee and bring forth my present, and set it before thee. And he said, I will tarry until thou come again.

And Gideon went in, and made ready a kid, and unleavened cakes of an ephah of flour: the flesh he put in a basket, and he put the broth in a pot, and brought it out unto him under the oak, and presented it.

And the angel of God said unto him, Take the flesh and the unleavened cakes, and lay them upon this rock, and pour out the broth. And he did so.

Then the angel of the Lord put forth the end of the staff that was in his hand, and touched the flesh and the unleavened cakes; and there rose up fire out of the rock, and consumed the flesh, and the unleavened cakes. Then the angel of the Lord departed out of his sight. And when Gideon perceived that he was an angel of the Lord, Gideon said, Alas, O Lord God! for because I have seen an angel of the Lord face to face. And the Lord said unto him, Peace be unto thee; fear not: thou shalt not die.

Judges 6:11-23

An angel announced to the wife of Manoah that she would bear a son who would be a Nazarite and deliver Israel from the Philistines. The angel confirmed his promise with Manoah

And the children of Israel did evil again in the sight of the Lord; and the Lord delivered them into the hand of the Philistines forty years.

And there was a certain man of Zorah, of

the family of the Danites, whose name was Manoah; and his wife was barren, and bare not. And the angel of the Lord appeared unto the woman, and said unto her, Behold now, thou art barren, and bearest not: but thou shalt conceive, and bear a son. Now therefore beware, I pray thee, and drink not wine nor strong drink, and eat not any unclean thing: for, lo, thou shalt conceive, and bear a son; and no razor shall come on his head: for the child shall be a Nazarite unto God from the womb: and he shall begin to deliver Israel out of the hand of the Philistines.

Then the woman came and told her husband, saying, A man of God came unto me, and his countenance was like the countenance of an angel of God, very terrible: but I asked him not whence he was, neither told he me his name: but he said unto me, Behold, thou shalt conceive, and bear a son; and now drink no wine nor strong drink, neither eat any unclean thing: for the child shall be a Nazarite to God from the womb to the day of his death.

Then Manoah intreated the Lord, and said, O my Lord, let the man of God which thou didst send come again unto us, and teach us what we shall do unto the child that shall be born. And God hearkened to the voice of Manoah; and the angel of God came again unto the woman as she sat in the field: but Manoah her husband was not with her. And the woman made haste, and ran, and shewed her husband, and said unto him, Behold, the man hath appeared unto me, that came unto me the other day. And Manoah arose, and went after his wife, and came to the man, and said unto him, Art thou the man that spakest unto the woman? And he said, I am. And Manoah said, Now let thy words come to pass. How shall we order the child, and how shall we do unto him? And the angel of the Lord said unto Manoah, Of all that I said unto the woman let her beware. She may not eat of any thing that cometh of the vine, neither let her drink wine or strong drink, nor eat any unclean thing: all that I commanded her let her observe.

And Manoah said unto the angel of the Lord, I pray thee, let us detain thee, until we shall have made ready a kid for thee. And the angel of the Lord said unto Manoah, Though thou detain me, I will not eat of thy bread: and if thou wilt offer a burnt offering, thou must offer it unto the Lord. For Manoah knew not that he was an angel of the Lord. And Manoah said unto the angel of the Lord, What is thy name, that when thy sayings come to pass we may do thee honour? And the angel of the Lord said unto him, Why askest thou thus after my name, seeing it is secret? So Manoah took a kid with a meat offering, and offered it upon a rock unto the Lord: and the angel did wondrously; and Manoah and his wife looked on. For it came to pass, when the flame went up toward heaven from off the altar, that the angel of the Lord ascended in the flame of the altar. And Manoah and his wife looked on it, and fell on their faces to the ground. But the angel of the Lord did no more appear to Manoah and to his wife. Then Manoah knew that he was an angel of the Lord.

Judges 13:1-21

An angel was about to bring destruction on Jerusalem but the Lord stayed the angel's hand. David saw the angel

And David said unto Gad, I am in a great strait: let us fall now into the hand of the Lord; for his mercies are great: and let me not fall into the hand of man.

So the Lord sent a pestilence upon Israel from the morning even to the time appointed: and there died of the people from Dan even to Beersheba seventy thousand men. And when the angel stretched out his hand upon Jerusalem to destroy it, the Lord repented him of the evil, and said to the angel that destroyed the people, It is enough: stay now thine hand. And the angel of the Lord was by the threshingplace of Araunah the Jebusite. And David spake unto the Lord when he saw the angel that smote the people, and said, Lo, I have sinned, and I have done wickedly: but these sheep, what have they done? let thine hand, I pray thee, be against me, and against my father's house.

2 Samuel 24:14-17

An angel provided Elijah with meat and drink that sustained him for forty days

But he himself went a day's journey into the wilderness, and came and sat down under a juniper tree: and he requested for himself that he might die; and said, It is enough; now, O Lord, take away my life; for I am not better than my fathers. And as

he lay and slept under a juniper tree,
behold, then an angel touched him, and said
unto him, Arise and eat. And he looked,
and, behold, there was a cake baken on the
coals, and a cruse of water at his head. And
he did eat and drink, and laid him down
again. And the angel of the Lord came again
the second time, and touched him, and said,
Arise and eat; because the journey is too
great for thee.

1 Kings 19:4-7

**An angel instructed Elijah to meet the
king's messengers and give them a
message for the king**

Then Moab rebelled against Israel after
the death of Ahab. And Ahaziah fell down
through a lattice in his upper chamber that
was in Samaria, and was sick: and he sent
messengers, and said unto them, Go, inquire
of Baalzebub the god of Ekron whether I
shall recover of this disease. But the angel
of the Lord said to Elijah the Tishbite,
Arise, go up to meet the messengers of the
king of Samaria, and say unto them, Is it
not because there is not a God in Israel,
that ye go to inquire of Baalzebub the god
of Ekron? Now therefore thus saith the

Lord, Thou shalt not come down from that bed on which thou art gone up, but shalt surely die. And Elijah departed.

2 Kings 1:1-4

An angel told Elijah not to fear meeting the king

And the angel of the Lord said unto Elijah, Go down with him: be not afraid of him. And he arose, and went down with him unto the king.

2 Kings 1:15

An angel struck the camp of the Assyrians outside Jerusalem, killing 185,000

And it came to pass that night, that the angel of the Lord went out, and smote in the camp of the Assyrians an hundred fourscore and five thousand: and when they arose early in the morning, behold, they were all dead corpses. So Sennacherib king of Assyria departed, and went and returned, and dwelt at Nineveh.

2 Kings 19:35-36

The Lord's angel saved and redeemed Israel

I will mention the lovingkindnesses of the Lord, and the praises of the Lord, according to all that the Lord hath bestowed on us, and the great goodness toward the house of of Israel, which he hath bestowed on them according to his mercies, and according to the multitude of his lovingkindnesses. For he said, Surely they are my people, children that will not lie: so he was their Saviour. In all their affliction he was afflicted, and the angel of his presence saved them: in his love and in his pity he redeemed them; and he bare them, and carried them all the days of old.

Isaiah 63:7-9

The Lord's angel delivered Shadrach, Meshach and Abednego

Then Nebuchadnezzar spake, and said, Blessed by the God of Shadrach, Meshach, and Abednego, who hath sent his angel, and delivered his servants that trusted in him, and have changed the king's word, and yielded their bodies, that they might not serve nor worship any god, except their own God.

Daniel 3:28

The Lord's angel shut the lions' mouths to protect Daniel

Then the king arose very early in the morning, and went in haste unto the den of lions. And when he came to the den, he cried with a lamentable voice unto Daniel: and the king spake and said to Daniel, O Daniel, servant of the living God, is thy God, whom thou servest continually, able to deliver thee from the lions? Then said Daniel unto the king, O king, live for ever. My God hath sent his angel, and hath shut the lions' mouths, that they have not hurt me: forasmuch as before him innocency was found in me; and also before thee, O king, have I done no hurt. Then was the king exceeding glad for him, and commanded that they should take Daniel up out of the den. So Daniel was taken up out of the den, and no manner of hurt was found upon him, because he believed in his God.

Daniel 6:19-23

An angel gave Daniel skill and understanding

Yea, whiles I was speaking in prayer, even the man Gabriel, whom I had seen in the vision at the beginning, being caused to fly swiftly, touched me about the time of the evening oblation. And he informed me, and talked with me, and said, O Daniel, I am now come forth to give thee skill and understanding. At the beginning of thy supplications the commandment came forth, and I am come to shew thee; for thou art greatly beloved: therefore understand the matter, and consider the vision.

Daniel 9:21-23

Angels ask questions and give a prophet answers

And the angel that talked with me came again, and waked me, as a man that is wakened out of his sleep, and said unto me, What seest thou? And I said, I have looked, and behold a candlestick all of gold, with a bowl upon the top of it, and his seven lamps thereon, and seven pipes to the seven lamps, which are upon the top thereof: and two olive trees by it, one upon the right side of the bowl, and the other upon the left side thereof. So I answered and spake to the angel that talked with me, saying, What are these, my lord? Then the angel that talked with me answered and said unto me, Knowest thou not what these be? And I said, No, my lord. Then he answered and spake unto me, saying, This is the word of the Lord unto Zerubbabel, saying, Not by might, nor by power, but by my spirit, saith the Lord of hosts. Who art thou, O great mountain? before Zerubbabel thou shalt become a plain: and he shall bring forth the headstone thereof with shoutings, crying, Grace, grace unto it. Moreover the word of the Lord came unto me, saying, The hands of Zerubbabel have laid the foundation of this house; his hands shall also finish it; and thou shalt know that the Lord of hosts hath sent me unto you. For who hath despised the day of small things? for they shall rejoice, and shall see the plummet in the hand of Zerubbabel with those seven; they are the eyes of the Lord, which run to and fro through the whole earth.

Then answered I, and said unto him, What are these two olive trees upon the right side of the candlestick and upon the left side thereof? And I answered again, and said unto him, What be these two olive branches which through the two golden pipes empty the golden oil out of themselves? And he answered me and said, Knowest thou not what these be? And I said, No, my lord. Then said he, These are the two anointed ones, that stand by the Lord of the whole earth.

Zechariah 4:1-14

VII. What the Gospels Say About the Activity of Angels in the Life of Jesus

An angel announced to Mary that she would conceive a son by the Holy Spirit who would be called the Son of the Highest

And in the sixth month the angel Gabriel was sent from God unto a city of Galilee, named Nazareth, to a virgin espoused to a man whose name was Joseph, of the house of David; and the virgin's name was Mary. And the angel came in unto her, and said, Hail, thou that art highly favoured, the Lord is with thee: blessed art thou among women. And when she saw him, she was

troubled at his saying, and cast in her mind
what manner of salutation this should be.
And the angel said unto her, Fear not, Mary:
for thou hast found favour with God. And,
behold, thou shalt conceive in thy womb,
and bring forth a son, and shalt call his
name Jesus. He shall be great, and shall be
called the Son of the Highest: and the Lord
God shall give unto him the throne of his
father David: and he shall reign over the
house of Jacob for ever; and of his kingdom
there shall be no end. Then said Mary unto
the angel, How shall this be, seeing I know
not a man? And the angel answered and
said unto her, The Holy Ghost shall come
upon thee, and the power of the highest
shall overshadow thee: therefore also that
holy thing which shall be born of thee shall
be called the Son of God. And, behold, thy
cousin Elisabeth, she hath also conceived a
son in her old age: and this is the sixth
month with her, who was called barren.
For with God nothing shall be impossible.
And Mary said, Behold the handmaid of the
Lord; be it unto me according to thy word.
And the angel departed from her.

Luke 1:26-38

In a dream an angel appeared to Joseph and told him about Mary's miraculous conception and that the Son would be called Jesus

Then Joseph her husband, being a just man, and not willing to make her a publick example, was minded to put her away privily. But while he thought on these things, behold, the angel of the Lord appeared unto him in a dream, saying, Joseph, thou son of David, fear not to take unto thee Mary thy wife: for that which is conceived in her is of the Holy Ghost. And she shall bring forth a son, and thou shalt call his name Jesus: for he shall save his people from their sins.

Matthew 1:19-21

The angel of the Lord came to shepherds and announced the birth of the Savior; then a multitude of angels appeared, praising God

And there were in the same country shepherds abiding in the field, keeping watch over their flock by night. And, lo, the angel of the Lord came upon them, and the glory of the Lord shone round about them: and they were sore afraid. And the angel said unto them, Fear not: for, behold, I bring you good tidings of great joy, which shall be to all people. For unto you is born this day in the city of David a Saviour, which is Christ the Lord. And this shall be a sign unto you; Ye shall find the babe wrapped in swaddling clothes, lying in a manger. And suddenly there was with the angel a multitude of the heavenly host praising God, and saying, Glory to God in the highest, and on earth peace, good will toward men. And it came to pass, as the angels were gone away from them into heaven, the shepherds said one to another, Let us now go even unto Bethlehem, and see this thing which is come to pass, which the Lord hath made known unto us.

Luke 2:8-15

In a dream an angel warned Joseph to flee to Egypt with Mary and baby Jesus

And when they were departed, behold, the angel of the Lord appeareth to Joseph in a dream, saying, Arise, and take the young child and his mother, and flee into Egypt, and be thou there until I bring thee word:

for Herod will seek the young child to destroy him.

Matthew 2:13

Angels ministered to Jesus after He was tempted by the devil

And he was there in the wilderness forty days, tempted of Satan; and was with the wild beasts; and the angels ministered unto him.

Mark 1:13

Then the devil leaveth him, and, behold, angels came and ministered unto him.

Matthew 4:11

An angel strengthened Jesus after He prayed, "not my will, but thine, be done"

And he was withdrawn from them about a stone's cast, and kneeled down, and prayed, saying, Father, if thou be willing, remove this cup from me: nevertheless not my will, but thine, be done. And there appeared an angel unto him from heaven, strengthening him. And being in an agony he prayed more earnestly: and his sweat

129

was as it were great drops of blood falling down to the ground.

Luke 22:41-44

Two angels in Jesus' empty tomb asked Mary why she was weeping

But Mary stood without at the sepulchre weeping: and as she wept, she stooped down, and looked into the sepulchre, and seeth two angels in white sitting, the one at the head, and the other at the feet, where the body of Jesus had lain. And they say unto her, Woman, why weepest thou? She saith unto them, Because they have taken away my Lord, and I know not where they have laid him.

John 20:11-13

An angel instructed the two Marys to announce Jesus' resurrection to His disciples

In the end of the sabbath, as it began to dawn toward the first day of the week, came Mary Magdalene and the other Mary to see the sepulchre. And, behold, there was a great earthquake: for the angel of the Lord descended from heaven, and came and rolled back the stone from the door, and sat upon it. His countenance was like lightning, and his raiment white as snow: and for fear of him the keepers did shake, and became as dead men. And the angel answered and said unto the women, Fear not ye: for I know that ye seek Jesus, which was crucified. He is not here: for he is risen, as he said. Come, see the place where the Lord lay. And go quickly, and tell his disciples that he is risen from the dead; and, behold, he goeth before you into Galilee; there shall ye see him: lo, I have told you.

Matthew 28:1-7

VIII. What the New Testament Says About the Activity of Angels in Human Lives

An angel appeared to Zacharias and told him his wife would bear a son who would go before the Christ in the spirit and power of Elijah

There was in the days of Herod, the king of Judaea, a certain priest named Zacharias, of the course of Abia: and his wife was of

the daughters of Aaron, and her name was
Elisabeth. And they were both righteous
before God, walking in all the commandments and ordinances of the Lord blameless.
And they had no child, because that
Elisabeth was barren, and they both were
now well stricken in years. And it came to
pass, that while he executed the priest's
office before God in the order of his
course, according to the custom of the
priest's office, his lot was to burn incense
when he went into the temple of the Lord.
And the whole multitude of the people
were praying without at the time of
incense. And there appeared unto him an
angel of the Lord standing on the right side
of the altar of incense. And when Zacharias
saw him, he was troubled, and fear fell
upon him. But the angel of the Lord said
unto him, Fear not, Zacharias: for thy
prayer is heard; and thy wife Elisabeth shall
bear thee a son, and thou shalt call his
name John. And thou shalt have joy and
gladness; and many shall rejoice at his birth.
For he shall be great in the sight of the
Lord, and shall drink neither wine nor
strong drink; and he shall be filled with the
Holy Ghost, even from his mother's womb.

And many of the children of Israel shall he turn to the Lord their God. And he shall go before him in the spirit and power of Elias, to turn the hearts of the fathers to the children, and the disobedient to the wisdom of the just; to make ready a people prepared for the Lord. And Zacharias said unto the angel, Whereby shall I know this? for I am an old man, and my wife well stricken in years. And the angel answering said unto him, I am Gabriel, that stand in the presence of God; and am sent to speak unto thee, and to shew thee these glad tidings. And, behold, thou shalt be dumb, and not able to speak, until the day that these things shall be performed, because thou believest not my words, which shall be fulfilled in their season.

Luke 1:5-20

Whenever an angel troubled the water in a pool called Bethesda, the first into the water was healed

Now there is at Jerusalem by the sheep market a pool, which is called in the Hebrew tongue Bethesda, having five porches. In these lay a great multitude of impotent folk, of blind, halt, withered,

133

waiting for the moving of the water. For an angel went down at a certain season into the pool, and troubled the water: whosoever then first after the troubling of the water stepped in was made whole of whatsoever disease he had.

John 5:2-4

An angel released the apostles from prison and instructed them to stand in the temple and speak the words of life

Then the high priest rose up, and all they that were with him, (which is the sect of the Sadducees,) and were filled with indignation, and laid their hands on the apostles, and put them in the common prison. But the angel of the Lord by night opened the prison doors, and brought them forth, and said, Go, stand and speak in the temple to the people all the words of this life. And when they heard that, they entered into the temple early in the morning, and taught. But the high priest came, and they that were with him, and called the council together, and all the senate of the children of Israel, and sent to the prison to have them brought. But when the officers came, and found them not in the prison, they returned, and told, saying, The prison truly found we shut with all safety, and the keepers standing without before the doors: but when we had opened, we found no man within.

Acts 5:17-23

An angel instructed Philip to leave the city of Samaria and go to Gaza

And the angel of the Lord spake unto Philip, saying, Arise, and go toward the south unto the way that goeth down from Jerusalem unto Gaza, which is desert. And he arose and went: and, behold, a man of Ethiopia, an eunuch of great authority under Candace queen of the Ethiopians, who had the charge of all her treasure, and had come to Jerusalem for to worship, was returning, and sitting in his chariot read Esaias the prophet. Then the Spirit said unto Philip, Go near, and join thyself to this chariot.

Acts 8:26-29

An angel appeared to Cornelius in a vision and instructed him to send for Peter, providing directions for finding him

There was a certain man in Caesarea called Cornelius, a centurion of the band called the Italian band, a devout man, and one that feared God with all his house, which gave much alms to the people, and prayed to God alway. He saw in a vision evidently about the ninth hour of the day an angel of God coming in to him, and saying unto him, Cornelius. And when he looked on him, he was afraid, and said, What is it, Lord? And he said unto him, Thy prayers and thine alms are come up for a memorial before God. And now send men to Joppa, and call for one Simon, whose surname is Peter: he lodgeth with one Simon the tanner, whose house is by the sea side: he shall tell thee what thou oughtest to do. And when the angel which spake unto Cornelius was departed, he called two of his household servants, and a devout soldier of them that waited on him continually; and when he had declared all these things unto them, he sent them to Joppa.

Acts 10:1-8

An angel released Peter from chains in prison, and led him outside

Now about that time Herod the king stretched forth his hands to vex certain of the church. And he killed James the brother of John with the sword. And because he saw it pleased the Jews, he proceeded further to take Peter also. (Then were the days of the unleavened bread.) And when he had apprehended him, he put him in prison, and delivered him to four quaternions of soldiers to keep him; intending after Easter to bring him forth to the people. Peter therefore was kept in prison: but prayer was made without ceasing of the church unto God for him. And when Herod would have brought him forth, the same night Peter was sleeping between two soldiers, bound with two chains: and the keepers before the door kept the prison. And, behold, the angel of the Lord came upon him, and a light shined in the prison: and he smote Peter on the side, and raised him up, saying, Arise up quickly. And his chains fell off from his hands. And the angel said unto him, Gird thyself, and bind on thy sandals. And so he did. And he saith unto him, Cast thy garment about thee, and follow me. And he went out, and followed him; and wist not that it was true which was done by the angel; but thought he saw a vision. When they were past the first and the second ward, they came unto the iron gate that leadeth unto the city; which opened to them of his own accord: and they went out, and passed on through one street; and forthwith the angel departed from him. And when Peter was come to himself, he said, Now I know of a surety, that the Lord hath sent his angel, and hath delivered me out of the hand of Herod, and from all the expectation of the people of the Jews. And when he had considered the thing, he came to the house of Mary, the mother of John, whose surname was Mark; where many were gathered together praying.

Acts 12:1-10

An angel appeared to Paul during a storm at sea and assured him he would appear before Caesar and that everyone on the ship would survive even though the ship would be lost

But after long abstinence Paul stood forth in the midst of them, and said, Sirs, ye should have hearkened unto me, and not have loosed from Crete, and to have gained this harm and loss. And now I exhort you to be of good cheer: for there shall be no loss of any man's life among you, but of the ship. For there stood by me this night the angel of God, whose I am, and whom I serve, saying, Fear not, Paul; thou must be brought before Caesar: and, lo, God hath given thee all them that sail with thee. Wherefore, sirs, be of good cheer: for I believe God, that it shall be even as it was told me. Howbeit we must be cast upon a certain island.

Acts 27:21-26

NOTES

NOTES

NOTES

NOTES

NOTES